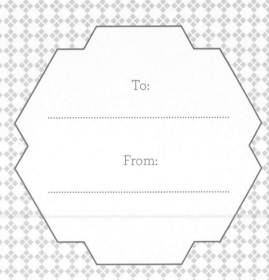

To:

....

From:

....

Other books in this series

Mother's Love

Love You, Dad

True Love

Friends Forever

The World Awaits

The Little Book of Thanks

A Gift of Joy and Appreciation

ANNE ROGERS SMYTH

NATIONAL GEOGRAPHIC

WASHINGTON, D.C.

PUBLISHED BY NATIONAL GEOGRAPHIC PARTNERS, LLC

1145 17th Street N.W., Washington, D.C. 20036

ISBN 978-1-4262-1551-3

Since 1888, the National Geographic Society has funded more than 12,000 research, exploration, and preservation projects around the world. National Geographic Partners distributes a portion of the funds it receives from your purchase to National Geographic Society to support programs including the conservation of animals and their habitats.

Get closer to National Geographic explorers and photographers, and connect with our global community. Join us today at nationalgeographic.com/join

For information about special discounts for bulk purchases, please contact National Geographic Books Special Sales: specialsales@natgeo.com

For rights or permissions inquiries, please contact National Geographic Books Subsidiary Rights: bookrights@natgeo.com

Interior design: Sanaa Akkach

Printed in China

19/RRDH/3

To my family,
a great big thank-you

Thank you for making life **one big treat.**

Pudgy-cheeked chipmunks are the smallest members of the squirrel family. Instead of storing fat for hibernation, they collect nuts and seeds to gnaw slowly through the winter.

Thank you for proving that **bolder** is better.

The macaw's vibrant plumage is suited to life in Central and South American rain forests, where these highly intelligent birds blend in with colorful fruits and flowers.

Thank you for noticing
the little things.

Male silverback mountain gorillas gain their silver tinge when they reach adulthood, at about 13 years old. With a genome sequence up to 98 percent identical to humans, gorillas are among our closest relatives.

Thank you for always **leveling** with me.

At an average of 6 feet (1.8 m), giraffes' legs alone are taller than many humans. They use their unrivaled height to graze on leaves that few other animals can reach, and they eat hundreds of pounds weekly.

Thank you for teaching me to catch whatever **life throws my way.**

Powerful and athletic, Great Danes are the tallest dogs in the world, reaching up to 3.5 feet (1.1 m) from paw to shoulder. Their affectionate nature earns them the designation "gentle giant."

Thank you for
sticking by my side.

Amazon milk frogs are so named for the poisonous, milky-white fluid they excrete when stressed. They hide in vegetation high above streams, aided by toe pads specially adapted to cling to branches.

Thank you for knowing how
to put a **smile** on my face.

Elephant calves weigh some 200 pounds (91 kg) at birth, having developed in a nearly two-year (22-month) gestation period. Their trunk alone contains about 10,000 different muscles.

Thank you for making
the whole world a **playground.**

Sea lions' streamlined bodies and strong flippers propel them through water and mobilize them on rocky terrain or sandy beaches. During deep-sea dives, they slow their heart rate to conserve oxygen.

Thank you for providing
a **comfort** that can't
be outgrown.

*Lions live in family units called prides, which include
up to three males, a dozen or so females who are all
related, and their young. All the lions work together
to hunt faster animals, like antelopes.*

Thank you for understanding
my **changing moods.**

Chameleons communicate by quickly changing color and controlling the hues of different body parts.
The brightness of stripes, for example, may signal how likely they are to approach rivals.

Thank you for always making room for **one more.**

Inhabiting wooded areas and big cities alike, raccoons will snack on whatever's available—from fruits, seeds, and birds' eggs to garbage bin delights. Their average life span in the wild is three years.

Thank you for getting
more brilliant with age.

*True to its name, the European Peacock butterfly bears a distinctive black, blue, and yellow eyespot
on each of its wings, much like the wooing eyespots found on a peacock's display feathers.*

Thank you for reminding me to enjoy **simple pleasures.**

Despite their reputation, pigs are quite clean and are among the smartest domesticated animals. Sometimes they roll in mud to cool off—hence the association with dirtiness.

Thank you for keeping
me **on my toes.**

Baby brown bears are usually born in pairs, blind and without hair. For up to two and a half years, they learn from and imitate their mother's methods for locating food before going to live on their own.

Thank you for your
undivided attention.

Great gray owls' asymmetrically set ear openings help them locate noises by using the time difference in which the sound is perceived in the right and left ear.

Thank you for
giving me **confidence.**

Hippos spend up to 16 hours a day submerged in water to cool their massive bodies from the hot African climate. On land, their bodies secrete an oily red substance that blocks the sun.

Thank you for
always maintaining
grace and composure.

Praying mantids have two large compound eyes with three
simple eyes centered between them, and they can turn their
heads 180 degrees to scan their surroundings.

Thank you for
staying **genuine.**

A smaller relative of camels and llamas, South American alpacas are valued for their fiber rather than their ability to bear loads. Their soft and durable hair is second only to mohair in strength.

Thank you for
moments of **sweetness.**

Normally solitary creatures, chipmunks will ignore one another until the spring, when females attract mates with a shrill, birdlike chirp. The young stay with their mothers for two months after birth.

Thank you for
fearless leadership.

❧

Gentoo penguins make as many as 450 dives a day to forage for fish, squid, and krill. They can remain underwater for up to seven minutes and swim at incredible speeds of as much as 22 miles an hour (35 kph).

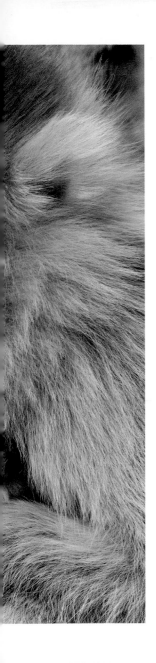

Thank you for warmth
like no other.

Found in the Qin Ling Mountains of central China, the snub-nosed monkey evolved to survive subzero temperatures. Its heavy fur and flat muzzle preclude the danger of frostbite to bare appendages.

Thank you for
knowing when it's
time for a breather.

*The name "aardvark" comes from South Africa's Afrikaans language
and means "earth pig." When digging for termites—a favorite food—
aardvarks close the nostrils of their piglike snouts for protection.*

Thank you for helping me **reach new heights.**

Land snails move by waves of muscular contractions that course up and down their single foot.
A layer of mucus helps them crawl over rough surfaces.

Thank you for showing me
unexplored corners.

❧

Agile Asian grass lizards emerge in the early morning to bask in the sun. Like geckos, they can drop their tails (up to three times the length of their bodies) and grow a new one if attacked.

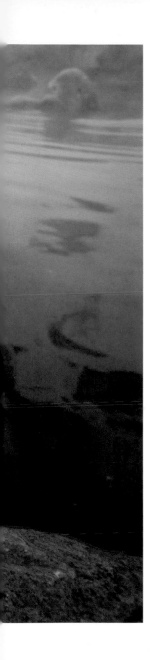

Thank you for
teaching me how
to let go **and relax.**

Living farther north than any other nonhuman primates,
Japanese macaques bathe in hot springs during freezing winters.
They are known for washing and flavoring their food with salt water.

Thank you for
endless conversation.

Puffins live mostly at sea, resting on the waves when they aren't swimming. Surprisingly swift,
they use their wings to stroke underwater and to fly—flapping up to 400 times per minute.

Thank you for **being ready** to come running.

The rapidly churning legs and the long, webbed toes on the rear feet of the green basilisk lizard enable it to dart across water—earning it the unmistakable nickname of Jesus Christ lizard.

Thank you for adding
a **spark** of mischief.

*Found in tropical oceans and other warm waters around the globe, bottlenose dolphins
have curved mouths that give the appearance of a permanent smile.*

Thank you for knowing when
to keep your **lips sealed.**

*With an average life span of more than 100 years, Galápagos tortoises lead relatively
simple lives: munching on grass, leaves, and cactuses and snoozing nearly 16 hours a day.*

Thank you for **inspiring me** to see things differently.

Sedentary feather duster worms wave their long, flowing appendages to create current that directs plankton their way. The colorful tentacles are key to survival.

Thank you for
respecting my space.

❧

Territorial Bengal tigers scent-mark their area to keep away rivals. At night they travel miles, tracking buffalo, deer, wild pigs, and other large mammals, then lie in wait for the perfect moment to pounce.

Thank you
for simple
moments made
extraordinary.

*Fur seals have sharp eyesight and hearing: Mothers
and pups find each other using a familiar call, some recog-
nizing each other's cry even after years of separation.*

Thank you for **staying flexible**
in any situation.

Nectar-loving fruit bats live in warm climates where fruit and flowers are abundant. They aid plant growth by carrying pollen between blossoms, or by spitting and eliminating fruit seeds.

Thank you for sharing the
best secrets.

Dachshund—German for "badger dog"—is a short-legged, long-bodied hound. Bred to hunt burrowing animals, they have paddle-shaped paws for digging and loose skin that won't tear while they are tunneling in tight spaces.

Thank you for knowing when
a hug is **worth more than words.**

Armed with an insulating layer of fat and thick fur, Arctic-dwelling polar bears roam the ice.
Their white coat blends in with the snow, but underneath is black skin that absorbs the sun's warming rays.

Thank you for **encouraging me** to charge ahead.

Wild horses gather in groups of 3 to 20 animals, with a stallion leading. When young males become colts at two years of age, the stallion drives them off until they can gather their own following.

Thank you for **love**
I can count on.

The distinctive bleats (or "baa" sound) of individual sheep help the ewe and her young recognize one another. They stick in close-knit flocks as they graze and seek new pasture.

Thank you for always
going with **the flow.**

The hawksbill sea turtle takes its name from its birdlike head and clawed flippers. The most dangerous time of its life is the journey from beach to sea after hatching, when crabs and birds prey.

Thank you for
effortless companionship.

Though often spotted in a relaxed sitting posture, pandas are strong swimmers and skilled tree-climbers. They may climb as high as 13,000 feet (4,000 m) to eat and cool off in China's bamboo forests.

Thank you for being **anything but boring.**

Known as the "chameleons of the sea," cuttlefish can change the color, pattern, and shape of their skin to communicate. Blue, red, yellow, brown, and black pigments produce a dazzling range of color.

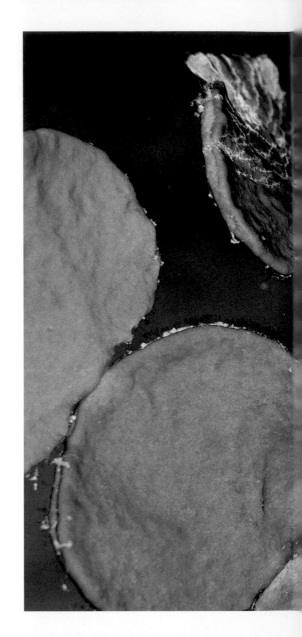

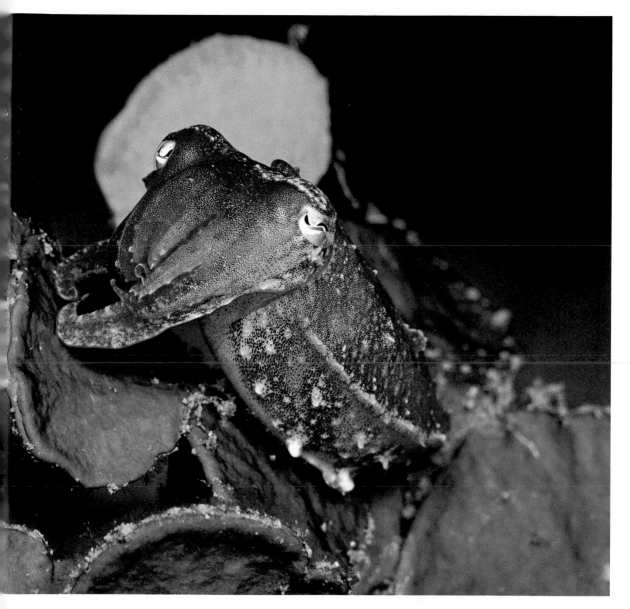

Thank you for being
up for anything.

The arctic fox's fur changes with the seasons, from a white or blue-gray winter camouflage to a brown or gray that matches the summer tundra. Its thick tail provides balance and warmth year-round.

Thank you for being my **perfect match.**

Zebra stripes may serve several functions: a form of camouflage that creates a confusing blur for predators when herds run together; a natural sunscreen that diffuses rays; or a means of identifying individuals.

Illustrations Credits

Cover, Tomokazu Yamada/Getty Images; 5, Eric Isselee/Shutterstock; 8-9, Lori Deiter/National Geographic Your Shot; 11, Super Prin/Shutterstock; 12-13, Ian Nichols/National Geographic Creative; 14, Martin Novak/Shutterstock; 17, Dmussman/Shutterstock; 18-19, George Grall/National Geographic Creative; 21, Klein-Hubert/Kimball Stock; 22-23, David Doubilet/National Geographic Creative; 24-25, Michael Nichols/National Geographic Creative; 26, Oxana Brigadirova/Fotolia; 29, Konrad Wothe/Minden Pictures; 30, Thomas Marent/Minden Pictures; 32-33, Neo Vision/Getty Images; 34-35, Daniel J. Cox/Kimball Stock; 36, Erni/Shutterstock; 39, Cesar Aristeiguieta/National Geographic Your Shot; 40-41, Yahya Taufikurrahman; 42, acceleratorhams/Fotolia; 45, Tom Reichner/Shutterstock; 46-47, Michael Lorentz/National Geographic Your Shot; 48-9, Cyril Ruoso/Minden Pictures; 50-51, Gary Parker/National Geographic Your Shot; 53, Yahya Taufikurrahman; 54-55, Yahya Taufikurrahman; 56-57, Tim Laman/National Geographic Creative; 59, Irene Becker Photography/Getty Images; 60-61, Bence Mate/Visuals Unlimited/Corbis; 62, Flip Nicklin/Minden Pictures; 65, Tim Laman/National Geographic Creative; 66-67, Chris Newbert/Minden Pictures; 68-69, Steve Winter/National Geographic Creative; 70-71, Yva Momatiuk & John Eastcott/Minden Pictures; 73, gallimaufry/Shutterstock; 74-75, Mark Raycroft/Minden Pictures; 76, Michio Hoshino/Minden Pictures; 78-79, Tina Thuell/National Geographic Your Shot; 81, Natalia Paklina/Shutterstock; 82, Rich Carey/Shutterstock; 85, fototrav/iStockphoto; 86-87, Chris Newbert/Minden Pictures; 88, Sergey Gorshkov/Minden Pictures; 90-91, Richard Du Toit/Minden Pictures; 93, Eric Isselee/Shutterstock; Back Cover, Neo Vision/Getty Images.